A journey through
the layers of your stuff
to the essence of your Self

simply enough

Create space for what matters

Dyan
Enjoy the journey into Simply Enough

Sora

Sora Garrett
Shine Publishing

Published by Shine Publishing,
an imprint of Inspired Connections, LLC
Star, Idaho USA

ISBN-13: 978-0-9969037-4-5

Cover & interior design by Jennifer Andrews

*A portion of every book sale is donated
in support of innovation & grassroots change.*

Group discounts available upon request.

For my parents,
who taught me simplicity.

For my family & friends,
who help me know enough.

For my grandson,
my more-than-enough.

Contents

Introduction

Life is a journey of accumulation.

...until it becomes an adventure

in letting go.

Another book about simplicity?

Yes, and to be honest, I almost didn't write this one. There are plenty of books to inspire you to simplify your spaces and bring a little sanity back to your life, even if you don't want to be a minimalist.

Those books are very good at helping you organize your spaces, get rid of excess, and live a more peaceful life...if you do more than just read them.

Then why did I decide to write this book?

Because I've been searching for the balance between having a simple life and taking care of some of the BIG problems of the world...and I thought others might be searching too.

The world needs our creativity and resourcefulness more than ever, and most of us are so overwhelmed by the constant clutter of life that we are barely keeping up with the basics, much less considering how we might contribute to a better world.

So, yes, this is a book about simplicity.

But it is also a book about complexity, a world of excess, the out-of-balance spaces in our lives that cause us to miss the things that are most important while being consumed by what is not.

Engaging in life is important. Spending time buried in clutter, too busy-stressed-overwhelmed to pay attention to your health and happiness, is not.

If you yearn for a simpler pace of life that is not quite so full of obligations, technology, and excess physical stuff, you are not alone.

If you are *also* wondering how your life might be more full of meaning and contribution, even as you let go of some of that excess, I invite you to keep reading.

This book is a bridge between these seemingly divergent lives, where clearing clutter opens space to be a solution for the world.

Can clearing clutter actually change the world?

Maybe. You may have noticed simplicity is a hot topic that appears to be reaching a tipping point. We are drowning in clutter and information overload. People are overwhelmed, exhausted, and unhappy. Some are depressed, others anxious.

Life is not simple.

While more connected than ever with what is happening around the world, we are possibly less connected than ever to our neighbors, and to our souls.

If you are not overly busy, you might think something is wrong with you because...how can you possibly have a full life without a full calendar?

I spent years as an over-achiever trying to unhook myself from this belief.

And what about our children? They are labeled hyperactive, when perhaps they are just reacting to an over-busy world, over-stimulated by all the choices, activities, technology, and processed foods.

I saw a two-year old playing on a tablet at a restaurant the other day and wanted to cry. I see young people staring at their phones instead of the sky and cringe.

Then I do the exact same thing and cringe even more.

I know it sounds harsh, but this is part of the reality of our world, and a big part of the reason I am so passionate about helping you simplify your life.

It doesn't really matter how organized you are, but if I can help you create a more spacious and meaningful life, together we just might bring a bit more balance to an out-of-balance world.

Like many, I've faced cycles of depression and overwhelm from not knowing what to do about the state of the world. I spent years trying to find something to care about after I had burnt out from trying to change things from a place of overwhelm and obligation.

While my heart was breaking over some of the things happening in the world, it was simultaneously breaking open as I peeled away the layers of clutter and busyness to find a new kind of contribution that springs from overflow and inspiration.

Which brought me to another reality: the one where we are called to quell the tide of craziness by saying NO to the excess and YES to a more sane way of living with less clutter and busy-ness, more space and meaning.

You are here, so you are likely making a choice to slow down enough to get in touch with what you love and what might be missing from your over-full life.

This is what will change the world.

Clearing physical clutter might simplify your life, at least until it comes back again. The world changing will happen when enough of us clear our lives of the less essential so we can attend to the more.

More meaning. More connection. More contribution.

This book is an invitation to go beneath the surface of your clutter into the essence of your life, to look for what may have gotten lost beneath the layers of everyday living.

Start with your house and your calendar. Clear the excess layers of clutter and busy-ness, and you will find more than empty organized space.

You may find a few physical treasures in your clearing, but the most important treasures you'll find will come later, after you feel how the outer spaciousness has opened more space on the inside.

This is where the real treasure hunt begins, when you stop looking to fill the space and allow yourself to *become* the space you are looking for.

Let's start with this idea. Simplicity is not easy.

In fact, it's rather difficult. It is much easier to let the clutter pile up in your living spaces, to consume too much, to allow your calendar to be overly full, to let the emails pile up in your inbox, and to let your mind run in circles the way minds like to do.

It takes much more energy to clear the clutter, to make conscious buying decisions and ongoing choices to stay less busy, to devote time to completing your list of projects and emails, and to quiet your overly active mind.

It takes intense commitment and ongoing focus to keep an even *moderately* simple life. *Why choose to simplify then?*

For one thing, when your life is more spacious, you have more time and freedom to do what you love. Clutter is not just something you trip over. It also creates stress in your mind and causes you to lose things.

So choose to simplify in order to have a more efficient, productive, and peaceful life.

More importantly, choose to simplify because the world needs you. You have something that is yours to give, and when you are too busy taking care of excess possessions and commitments, you won't have the time or energy to give it.

When we get rid of the distractions and peel away the excess layers, we can move with more peaceful power into whatever world need is calling in any given moment.

The world has more than enough problems.

What if we have everything we need to solve them, buried beneath the unnecessary clutter of our everyday lives?

But what if I have enough problems of my own?

I know it seems rather bold to begin a simplicity book talking about solving world problems. Most of us have plenty to do without taking on changing the world.

So take a deep breath and stay with me, please.

The solution to all our problems begins with knowing we have enough to handle whatever comes. And that is so much easier when we have plenty of time and energy to pay attention to what is most essential.

Life is complex enough without adding to it by holding on to what we don't need, spending time on what we don't love, and getting overwhelmed by the clutter that is everywhere.

We are bombarded by information, technology, and endless opportunities to fill our calendars, not to mention the constant inflow of commitments and things to care for in our everyday lives.

Life can be overwhelming.

I'm not advocating that you add the burden of changing the world to your already overly full life. I simply invite you to slow down, pay attention to what you have accumulated, and consider where LESS might create even MORE in your life.

Less to take care of, more to care about.

If you have found this book, you are likely looking for something a little different to help navigate the complicated waters of life. I hope this will be that for you.

I'd like this to be a book that opens you, as you open it. I'd like it to give you some ideas for making your life more of what you love, while at the same time it expands your heart and calls you to give more of yourself to the world.

I'd like this book to help you clear what you no longer need so you can find the key to a more abundant life that is less about having belongings, and more about knowing where you belong.

Let's go beneath the layers of your life to find the ultimate treasure of a life well-lived from the depth of your love.

A few tips for getting the most from this book.

This book is a blend of inquiry, information, reflection, exploration, and practice. The flow between poetic and practical is intended to guide you deeper and create more lasting impact.

Simplifying and clearing clutter is a process, so don't overwhelm yourself by trying to read the book in one sitting. This book will create more impact if you actually do the activities, though it is perfectly fine to simply read and integrate the ideas if you are not in need of the practical support.

The opening poems and stories will breathe some space into your busy mind, even before you are ready to clear any physical clutter.

The 'pause' between each section is a reminder to give space within your own process. When you see a flower, take a deep breath, let go, and be grateful.

The questions are designed to take you through your own layers, but please LET GO of thinking you need to answer them all! Choose those that are most meaningful right now, and be willing to come back later for another layer.

I encourage you to use a journal to keep track of your insights as you go, and it might be both effective and fun for you to bring a couple of friends along for the journey. (Start a simplicity group, or join one of mine. ;-)

Most of all, enjoy the process of moving through the layers of this book to discover what is beneath your own layers. Have fun!

The Joy is in the Journey

May yours be full of delight.

Gathering

Having and Being Enough

Every journey begins with a single step.

Before you take your next step,

where are you now

...and where did you get

all that stuff?

There is a treasure in you...
a deep quiet that surrounds
all the shiny objects stored
in the crevices of your life.

Here, in this still center
is where the adventure begins:
a hunt for the diamond
that is the essence of You.

Open your heart wide in wonder,
seek beneath the surface to find
what you didn't even know
you were looking for.

Let simplicity be your guide
when the clutter of the world
begins to crowd your true identity
and dampen your joy.

Let go of everything if you need to,
just hold on tight to what you love.

Now let even that go.

When it comes back,
you'll know it's Real.

A lifetime of clutter

When you think of gathering, what images come to mind?

I see bushel baskets of produce, a woman filling her apron with flowers, a room filled with people who have come together for some special purpose.

None of those images makes me think of too much. They simply inspire feelings of joyful abundance and happiness.

Where, then, does gathering become too much?

If we collect more produce than we can eat or share with our neighbors, it can become rotten and wasted. If we forget to put the flowers in water, they will wilt and die. If we gather too many people into a small room, it becomes stifling and what was meant as a joyful occasion becomes just crowded and irritating.

Most of us begin thinking about simplicity after we've gathered way too much and begun to realize all that stuff is crowding or even suffocating us.

Perhaps it begins with a spring clean, something we were taught to do as a child, giving away old clothes that no longer fit or toys we haven't played with for some time...and it feels so good that we keep going.

Or we move and wonder how we managed to fit so many boxes into a single life, and begin to realize that most of what we are holding onto and storing is not really necessary for the life we want to live now.

Or we simply change, and at some point realize we have accumulated too many of the wrong things, and it's time to let go of the pieces that no longer define who we are becoming.

simply enough

Whatever the beginning, it usually has to do with clearing layers of clutter.

What if, instead, we begin by looking at where those layers came from in the first place?

Learning to Gather

When I came into this life, I had nothing except my naked awareness that this life might be a bit noisy for me. My mother says I
used to cringe in my crib when my father raised his voice, turning
away from a sound that was bombarding my newborn senses.

Perhaps that was when I started growing the shell that I thought
would protect me. Or maybe later, when my father encouraged
me to pick the stinging nettles in a misguided attempt to teach
me what they were. It worked, but I was left thinking I needed an
extra layer of protection from the harshness of the world.

Still, for the most part, my early years were simple and free. I
didn't have excess, yet life was very abundant.

We were a family of six living on a teacher's salary. My mother
chose a career as a stay-at-home mom, and I am so grateful for
the security that gave me. We spent our days playing games,
camping, reading, and making music. It was a mostly idyllic
childhood, and I have many happy memories from that phase
of my life.

We lived simply on a one-parent salary, and it was always
enough. Even so, my early years taught me to gather more than
I really needed.

As a highly sensitive child with a somewhat insensitive father, I
learned to gather layers of protection.

As one of four children vying for her parent's attention, I learned
to make sure I got my share. A seed of 'not-enough-so-I-must-
compete-to-get-my-share' was planted.

I had plenty, but still wanted more.

Then I entered school and started feeling the judging and sorting that happens when we begin to grow up. I'm sure most of you can relate. Childhood, especially the teen years, is anything but simple. I was also highly creative, so I got really good at adjusting myself to fit in, adapt, be liked, and play well with others.

But somewhere in the process of learning to fit in, I put on layers of other, then felt inadequate because I wasn't allowing my full self to shine through. This is where I began to think *I* wasn't enough, which taught me to keep gathering so I could have, do, and be even *more than* enough.

If you have ever tried to fit someone else's definition or expectation of what is enough, you will always fall short of your true essence. We can only BE enough when we are exactly who we are meant to BE.

To Be (or not to Be) Enough

So, there in my normal, mostly idyllic childhood, the seed got planted that to BE enough, I needed to prove myself. Later, proving myself became accumulating: grades, awards, roles, possessions, and accomplishments that would show how I was even *more than enough* because of all I had done, created, earned, gathered.

I became driven and highly effective at getting what I wanted, as well as a perfectionist, good at balancing a large number of responsibilities and roles. I gathered a lot of both.

I didn't want to be left out of anything, so I said yes to everything.

I moved into my mothering years at the same time I was finding myself in business and marriage. How can anyone hold all those roles without letting something drop? Like most mothers, I dropped self-nourishment. After my children left home, I finally began the process of rediscovering the inner essence I had covered little by little through the years.

Your growing up story may be similar or completely different, but it has likely impacted your relationship with what you have gathered, how you fill your time, and your sense of having/being enough.

Whether you experienced plenty or lack, you have developed some impression of what is enough, and what is not.

Even if you started on a path of simplicity early in life, you may have accumulated some beliefs around the idea of enough, perhaps even that having *too much* is wrong.

This book is not about right or wrong. It is simply inviting you to look at your relationship with what you have accumulated, then helping you consider whether you might be ready to change your relationship with it in order to create more space, happiness, and freedom in the way you spend your days.

There is nothing wrong with gathering. It's a natural part of life. We absolutely need to accumulate life experience to become who we are meant to be, and the result of those experiences is often more stuff.

But when those layers of accumulated belongings, beliefs, and obligations begins to get in the way of our happiness, productivity, relationships, and success...it's time to let go.

So take an honest look at what you have gathered.

Reflect: What am I Gathering?

Take a tour through your possessions. Walk through your home as if you are a non-judging visitor simply witnessing what is here. Look at all your physical belongings, including those in hidden spaces (drawers/boxes/closets).

Now sit with a journal & cup of tea, and consider these questions:

Which of my belongings make me most happy?

What do my physical belongings say about me?

Are any of my possessions no longer aligned with who I am becoming?

That's all for now. Simply notice what you have gathered through your life and how the various items make you feel.

You'll have a chance to sort your belongings later.

After you take an honest (non-judging) look through what you have gathered, come with me on a journey into the heart of your life. Because until you know what truly matters where you are right now, you won't know what you truly need to get where you are going.

Getting Clear on What Matters

When you took a tour of your spaces and your physical belongings, what felt most precious to you?

Was it the memories invoked, a sense of freedom you felt from how you might use something, a feeling of beauty/joy/love or some other positive emotion that was stimulated as you looked at what you have gathered?

If you need to, take another tour to get in touch with the deeper meaning attached to your stuff. Notice the essence of your relationship to what you have gathered. This is what matters. Not the possessions. You can almost always gather more.

Most of us, if faced with a life-threatening situation, could fit our most meaningful possessions inside a suitcase or car. During the fires and floods and earthquakes of recent years, many have been forced to do this.

Hopefully you and I won't have to make that choice, but it can be quite freeing to consider what we would actually walk away from if we had to.

When I look through all I've accumulated, even after doing major clutter clearing, there are few things I couldn't part with. I keep most of my physical possessions not because I absolutely need them, but because they invoke a positive feeling.

I am (mostly) unattached to the objects, because I know they are mere representations of what is more valuable to me: a memory, a connection, a sense of security, a feeling of joy or abundance.

But I am very clear that I could give away most of my belongings in a minute, if I had to. You could too.

So why is it still so hard to clear the non-meaningful clutter when it comes down to cleaning the garage, emptying a storage unit, or even giving away the clothes we have outgrown?

How do we actually learn to let go of what doesn't matter so we can spend more time and energy on what does?

Does it really matter that we only keep what makes us happy?

Only if our stuff is getting in the way of our happiness.

My Journey to Simple

My family did much to protect me from the harsh reality of a world biased toward people who don't go into sensory overload from too much external stimulation. I didn't understand how to let my tenderness thrive in this world, so I built a shell...then got busy collecting a lot of love, because I was going to need it where I was going.

When I was young, collecting love was trying to please my parents, and later my friends, as I strived to be popular. Without knowing it, I began to put on a few masks in order to fit in.

I was an achiever, so in addition to collecting friendship and love, I also collected good grades, sports ribbons, and other accomplishments that showed the world what a well-adjusted, well-rounded, successful person I was becoming. For the most part, this was true, but underneath the surface, feelings of not quite belonging silently simmered.

The pattern of collecting love and accomplishment went on into adulthood, where I married an amazing man, started a career at a well-respected high-tech company, created two remarkable children, helped launch several alternative schools, and began to gather physical possessions in pursuit of the American dream.

But striving to fit in and BE enough when you are a highly sensitive, creative person who really doesn't fit society's mold can be exhausting.

Striving to be enough, to have enough, to do enough can only lead to one place: burnout. When we juggle so many roles in an effort to be enough and have enough, eventually something has to drop. For me, it was the corporate career.

At the time, it felt like a natural choice to leave my high-paying job at a high-tech company to follow my heart and go after what mattered more to me than security and a good paycheck.

My children mattered. My creativity mattered. My passion to make a bigger difference in the world mattered. The corporate world had grown too small for me and I was ready to spread my entrepreneurial wings.

To be honest, I didn't really think I was giving anything up, though I was definitely moving away from a secure job and more stable financial situation. It was really more of a choice to move toward something that was calling, from deep in my soul, even though I had no idea what that was.

As I look back, this life choice was one of the first steps onto the road less travelled into a more simple life, but not until I had received quite a few lessons in letting go and a couple of significant opportunities to experience the pain of 'not' enough.

I'll share a few of those lessons later, but first I would like to invite you to look at another layer of questions to get clear on what matters most in *your* life.

What feels simple to one person may feel too much, or too little, to another. We each have our own threshold of spaciousness, and everyone's relationship with clutter looks different.

If you are reading this book, you are likely ready for a more spacious, clutter-free, meaning "full" life at some level.

To create lasting change, you will want to get crystal clear on what matters, as this is the touchstone that will keep you going when things get tough.

Because nobody said having a simple life was going to be easy.

To keep or not to keep.

We all have different needs and wants, so the journey to a more simple life will look different for everyone. I have friends who have sold most of their possessions to live in tiny houses or take up the RV life. Others still live in large homes with rooms full of art and an abundance of possessions.

I live somewhere in between.

My husband and I chose to move to a smaller home in order to pay off our mortgage and live debt-free. I have never missed the extra space and am in love with the way our right-sized home feels, a blend of art and organization, simple yet cozy.

Whatever size your life is, simplicity can still be an elusive thing, and clearing physical clutter is just ONE part of the solution.

Remember, this book isn't advising you to get rid of everything to live the life of a minimalist. That may be a destination for some, but most of us will continue to live with possessions we enjoy within homes we love. We will likely continue to have more space than we need and attract more stuff than we use.

This book is about creating spaces, inside and out, that leave plenty of room for connecting with what you *do* love, and about being mindful of what will contribute most to the life you are ready to live NOW.

As you clear some of the physical layers, your definition of simplicity may even change. Mine has.

While I have gradually let go of possessions, I have also gone through a mid-life transitioning to a more simple presence. I continually cull layers of stuff to keep clutter at bay, but inner peace is my ultimate goal.

As I grow through this exploration, my needs are shifting and what I desire and decide to keep is changing too.

It will likely be the same for you, so begin where you are and be gentle with yourself if you are not ready to release everything at once.

Your heart will know what to cling to and what to let go.

Listen.

simply enough

Practice: Knowing What to Keep

It's time to get practical. Sometimes I start my physical clutter-clearing as part of the process of deciding what is most important, but rarely do I make real progress until my heart is full of the essence of what I want to keep.

For me, this usually means spending less time having to maintain and deal with the excess stuff I have accumulated.

We all do this: vow to not buy another piece of clothing, shiny kitchen utensil, on-sale book, or any other new item we might for a brief moment think we need. But the piles begin to grow and our time is spent sorting and getting rid of things that are in the way. Our money is spent on trivial things that could have been so much more useful donated to a worthy cause. Our emotions are cluttered from feelings of guilt, worry, and regret.

Do yourself a favor and don't start clearing your outer layers until you have gotten clear on what you want to keep.

Once you connect with the essence of what truly matters to you, you'll know which of your belongings matter too. If something evokes a memory full of love or happiness, cling to that. Consider letting go of the rest.

What do you want to keep?

Make space and time in your life for this.

Reflect

Take another look at the Reflection Questions from pg 32.

Make a JOY LIST of the belongings that make you most happy.

As you go through the layers of releasing clutter, return to this list often. Let your JOY LIST be a reminder of the destination, and what you want to keep for the journey.

Now make a CLUTTER LIST of the possessions and areas of your life that feel heavy or burdensome.

Take this list out when you begin to feel overwhelmed by life's clutter. It will help you see some tangible steps you can take to lighten your life.

Release

Choose 3 things from your CLUTTER LIST to give away.

Give to someone you know who will appreciate the gift...or to a thrift store where it will find a new home.

The Deeper Questions

Which of my belongings are most connected to my identity and sense of self?

How would losing all (or most) of my possessions impact me?

Deep Cleaning

If you'd rather stick with surface cleaning, you can skip this section; but deep cleaning is where you'll find the treasures. So grab a cup of tea and your journal.

Take a few minutes to map the key segments of your life: early years, school, significant work/service events, marriage, family, etc. Now make a few bullet highlights about what each phase of your life gave to you.

I'm not suggesting you list the physical items you still have from each major life phase, although that might be an interesting exercise too.

Begin with what you learned...the key lessons that each part of your life taught you.

Were there any important teachers that helped you with these lessons?

Was there an important challenge that made you who you are today?

Were there any significant moments that changed the trajectory of your life?

What were the times you had enough...more than enough...not enough?

Spend as much time as you need, but do not over-think this. Simply breathe into your heart, notice what is there, and greet the memories with gratitude.

When I did this exercise, as part of writing this book, I saw a few general trends and repeating life lessons, as well as the times I began hanging on too tightly.

Most of us have patterns we carry with us through the various phases of our lives. When we make time to see the patterns, it can be easier to know what is essential. Then we can learn how to let go of that which is not.

Let's look a bit deeper into the essence of Enough.

One person's clutter is another's treasure.

What is weighting you down,
might set someone else free.

Sorting

Essence of Enough

What do you most need
to get to where you are going?

Take 3 deep breaths, and
remember to pack the essentials.

What is Enough?

Adequate. Sufficient.
As much as necessary.
Meeting expectations.

How much water does a flower need?
Is a cactus less thirsty than a daffodil?

What is Enough?

Somewhere between plenty and scarce,
abundant and lack, prosperity and poverty.
A feeling of satisfaction.

When does an empty stomach become full?
How is it possible for need to turn into greed?

Do I have enough?
Have I done enough?
Am I enough?

What IS Enough?

Finding Essence

The first time I traveled to Mexico, my heart broke as I saw children begging in the streets and families living in houses that most Americans would consider a backyard shed. Then I looked closer and saw a simple joy and engagement with life that many with an abundance of possessions never experience.

I wrote a poem at the time called "Poverty Eyes" that astonished me in its message. I was the one with poverty, as I was judging what I was seeing through a limited lens...a lens of my limited experience that had nothing to do with what I was seeing on the surface.

A lot has changed since that first trip outside of my privileged life, and at times I still feel poor compared to some of the people I meet in my travels.

Yes, there are still many parts of the world where a redistribution of resources would help support a better dignity of life. There are still people living without basic needs, and these are the problems we can solve when we clear enough space in our lives to see where we can help.

But even in the poorest countries in the world, most people still have enough. Many of those people lead rich lives full of spirit and simple joy.

At the same time, people in the countries with the most material possessions often lead impoverished lives full of worry, stress, and fear of loss.

I know it is never this simple, but my point is that the essence of enough has nothing to do with how much you have on the outside.

You will never have enough until you know you already have everything you need. The essence of enough has everything to do with what you have on the inside.

The dictionary uses some of the same words to define enough and essential. The words are similar, but the meaning of essential goes deeper.

Enough denotes a sense of adequacy. Essential goes to the heart of what is truly important. To get to the essence requires us to peel away the surface wants, to feel into what is calling us to do more than just exist.

The essence is what the Soul needs in order to truly live.

What is most essential to you?

If you are a musician, it may be your instrument. If you are an artist, it will be your paints or clay or whatever canvas you can find.

If you are a natural-born teacher, you will always need your students. If you are a humanitarian, your life will not be complete unless you are finding a way to serve a greater cause.

Maybe your cause is your family, and serving them is more important than anything else you could do.

At the essence of every one of us, there is a spark of something great. When you find yours, do not hold back.

Think beyond the basics into the heart of your joy.

You can have whatever your heart desires.

Just get rid of the rest.

Never Enough

It can be challenging to let ourselves be happy with a simple, joyful life when there are still so many things wrong in the world.

This is the intersection between being a spiritual seeker and a humanitarian activist, the heart of this book. I have spent years exploring both of these dimensions and have found no simple answers for how to live with equal attention to both.

When I am fully connected to my spiritual beingness, I feel utterly simple and perfectly enough. When I look around at the great need in the world, I feel never even close to enough.

I am absolutely committed to putting my spiritual awareness to work for the world. This is the whole reason I'm so passionate about helping people clear layers of clutter so I (and we) can give more attention to what IS essential, which is about creating a better world.

I've traveled countless miles in my journey to create a more compassionate world, igniting many projects for innovation and social change along the way.

When I got burnt out trying to change the outside world, I turned within and started the intricate dance of changing myself. This is the spiritual journey—within.

And while I've never forgotten or totally abandoned my activism, I did seem to put it on hold for a time. While I continue to donate to causes I believe in, I became more of a quiet observer of what is going on in the outside world.

I justified this with a belief that I was doing more by helping myself and others awaken, but honestly it was more about being disillusioned and overwhelmed by all the need.

simply enough

The world is beautiful, but it's also a huge mess.

I don't have all the answers for how to keep a perfect balance, aligned with spirit and gracefully showing up to give where the world needs us to give.

I do know that we will each find our own answers, and we will have the energy to do exactly what we are meant to do, as well as the courage to be fully and completely who we need to be, when we get rid of the distractions, the excess, and the less significant parts of our everyday lives.

For me, that belief is the constant motivation to keep peeling away the unnecessary layers. When they aren't there, I can move with more peaceful power into whatever world need is calling in any given moment.

Hungry children. Dirty water. Broken school systems. Sex traffic. Abuse at every level, people and environment. Disease. Pollution.

We are not intended to be knocked down by these needs, unless it is to our knees in prayer. We are intended to be moved, with passion and creative solutions, to change what we can when something is breaking our heart.

Your heart will show you what is essential.

Pay attention, then clear a path so you can do something. Do what you can, with what you have, whenever you can. It may not ever feel like enough, but it could be exactly what someone else needs in that moment.

This is the way we solve the problems of the world, one small act of love and compassion at a time.

Return to Essence

So what does it feel like to have exactly enough?

To a starving child, it might be a full stomach; to a starving artist, perhaps a bit more.

It is hard for me to even imagine life without plenty, where extra food is stored in the pantry and refrigerator, where extra clothes, more than I can ever wear, hang in the closet and fill my dresser drawers.

When I began this book, it was an attempt to find my own way through the idea that excess can, at some point, begin to detract from a life of ease and grace. Now, as I consider what it might be to live on the other side of enough, that is actually quite difficult to grasp.

What is the essence of enough?

If gathering inspires images of baskets of fruit, aprons of flowers, rooms full of people, what images portray a sense of just enough?

We are shown images of starving children and families whose lives have been devastated by some kind of disaster, yet most of you reading this book will likely never have to experience going days without food or clean water.

Our basic needs are met, and now our attention can shift to whether or not we have enough to meet our future needs, not only the necessities of the moment. So all we can do is imagine the spectrum between lack and plenty, then find the level that feels right and good.

What may seem like not enough to one person, can feel like

bounty to another. Where one person may see lack, another feels the glow of spacious possibility.

You will find your sense of "just enough" through practice and trusting your inner guidance.

Whatever you find, it will likely keep changing, but here is what I invite you to keep: the essence of life is here for you, in every precious moment, and nothing you own is going to help you live there more completely.

Reflect: What is Enough...for me?

Think again of the various phases/stages of your own life story, from childhood to wherever you are right now. Without getting too caught up in the memories and the stories, make time with your simplicity journal to answer whichever questions inspire you.

Where in my life was there enough...and where was there lack?

When did I feel most free and happy...and how did those parts of my life impact my beliefs about having or being enough?

Are any of those stories/beliefs causing me to hang onto more than I need?

What do I really need?

Now that you have had time to consider what matters, can you see how clearing some of your stuff might uncover more time and space for what is more meaningful?

Let's go one step deeper into clutter, then it will be time to start sorting some of those layers.

The Clutter of Limiting Beliefs

Do you ever feel like your mind is even more cluttered than your closets? It's bound to be, with all the years of information pouring in and layers of judgments and beliefs picked up along the way.

Your brain is a huge storage bin of miscellaneous paraphernalia, sorted into a unique, personalized closet labeled simply: my life.

Getting to the essence of what we want to keep is partly about sorting through the habits and thought-patterns that keep us accumulating, not only the physical layers, but also thoughts and ideas that are not useful.

Have you ever thought...

> *But what if I throw away something I might need some day?*

> *What if I decide to finish that creative project I've been thinking about for the past 5 years?*

> *What if I lose this extra 10 pounds I've put on and need the clothes that are still hanging in my closet but too tight to comfortably wear?*

Perhaps you are hanging onto something, not because you love and use it, but because you are worried about not having it for (insert whatever reason you might have).

Or you might be saving something, not because it is truly special to you and makes you happy, but because someone gave it to you and you feel obligated to keep it.

Like most of us, you probably have a few belongings kept as a safety net for that 'some day' you might find a use for them.

Probably 80% of what we hold onto is excess baggage.

However much of that baggage consists of too-many physical possessions, it's likely that *more* of the clutter exists in your mind.

So the first step in any clutter-clearing endeavor is to adjust our beliefs.

Ohhhhhh noooooo. Don't take my beliefs away!!!

Don't worry. I know there are piles of books already trying to do that, and if you are hanging on too tightly, nothing you read is going to considerably change what you believe to be true.

So please, hold onto your beliefs (if they are serving you) and pretty please do *not* layer other people's beliefs on top of your own. This is one of the ways we accumulate so much mind clutter in the first place.

I only want to encourage you to pay attention to your thoughts as you go through the process of clearing your physical layers. Notice where your thoughts are crowded and where they are spacious.

What does spacious thinking feel like?

To me, it feels light, open and free, full of possibility.

Like a garden might feel after you till the weeds and prepare the soil for new seedlings.

Or how you might feel when you look at the sun rising against the backdrop of a clear mountain lake, reflections of expansive beauty in your eyes.

simply enough

Spacious thinking creates an opening for wonder and positive solutions that come from a place beyond the conscious, often-limited, brain.

Crowded thinking is stuck on a belief or way of seeing something that doesn't allow other perspectives to even be considered.

Spacious thinking is less about what you *should* do, and more about where your heart is calling.

Crowded thinking is when the mind won't shut off and keeps circling around the same stuff, over and over. (Kind of like moving piles of clutter around because you can't decide where they belong.)

Spacious thinking allows your creativity to flourish and intuition to ignite.

Meditation, stillness, and long walks in nature are great ways to empty and return to spacious thinking.

Another way is to listen closely, to notice where your thoughts are limiting you, and to look at where you might open to a more spacious way of believing.

Getting Spacious with your Thoughts

I learned about spacious thinking through my friend Julaine, a beacon of unlimited possibility. She had a way of opening minds with her questions and way of seeing the world as full of potential just waiting to be discovered. She lived her life fully, peering into the perfection of the universe, truly believing everything is possible when we unlimit our minds.

When I first met her, Julaine had just moved from east to west, and she was transforming her "Center for Unlimited Possibilities" from a physical space to one that lived in her heart. A few powerful expressions defined how she lived her life:

Everything is Perfect. She looked for the perfection in whatever life gave her, even if it was a perceived difficulty at the time. She assumed it was there for a reason, then focused on how she might learn and grow from whatever was happening.

When you look at the perfection of life this way, everything is a gift and things tend to show up to prove you right.

We are each a Center of Unlimited Possibility. Julaine's abbreviation for her physical Center was C.U.P. and she taught people to fill their own cup by receiving positive daily nourishment for both mind and body.

The best way to stay open to possibility is by filling to overflow with positive thoughts and habits.

Life is an Adventure. Julaine lived fully, taking new classes and always having something new to share with her weekly Blessing group. When she traveled, which was often, she would take along puppets, making friends with the local children while giving away smiles and laughter everywhere she went.

simply enough

Even her passing was an adventure. She died in an accident with her husband of 50 years, and their car was found near Idaho's Rainbow Bridge, which is where she had always told her children and grandchildren their beloved pets would be waiting. This helped her loved ones remember the blessing of their lives, even as they grieved the loss.

When we open our thinking, even death becomes an adventure into something greater.

This is a touching story, but how can believing in unlimited possibility possibly make it easier to sort through all the layers of stuff to discover what is most essential?

And, what does unlimited possibility even have to do with getting rid of excess?

Good questions.

Let me start with a disclaimer. I don't actually believe everything is unlimited. It makes me angry to see humans treating the earth as if it is disposable, and I know there are a lot of unconscious beliefs that are wasting resources that may drastically impact our future generations.

I am obsessive about repurposing, recycling, and limiting my use of resources that are not without limits. I beg you to be conscious about the impact you are having on the earth. Denying those limited resources is not the unlimited thinking I am suggesting.

What I do suggest is that you consider where you are hanging onto more than you need because of some level of limited thought, as well as where you might open even more possibility in your life by opening more space in your mind.

This book will guide you through layers of clearing both physical and mental clutter, but the lasting change will only come as you learn to create more spacious thinking, starting with unlimiting your beliefs.

For example...

> *If you have lost everything at some point in life, or have struggled to just survive, you may believe you need more physical possessions to feel safe and secure.*

> *If you had to work extra hard to gather what you have, and you believe your worth is somehow connected to what you gathered, it may be extra difficult to let go of things that are tied to your identity.*

> *If your cultural conditioning equates success with having...if your family sees material wealth as a sign of security...if you buy into any of the American dream where more is better...well, you get the picture.*

On the other hand...

> *If you believe you can create anything—that you are an endless ongoing resource of creative potential— you will know that everything you have gathered is an example of this. You will know that you can always create it again.*

When you believe anything is possible, it is much easier to quit hanging onto what you don't need. When you know life itself is moving and changing and always opening to new possibility, you have less reason to dwell in the old.

Do you resonate with any of these limiting beliefs? It might be time to do a bit of clutter clearing to find a few more...

simply enough

Practice: One Box and Belief at a Time

It's time to get physical. It can be overwhelming to look at limiting beliefs and decide what we truly want to keep, so the best way to start is by beginning to clear the obvious clutter.

We all have it, so find yours and start clearing.

Reflect

Physical: Where are my physical belongings taking up space that could be open to new possibility? Could others benefit from any of the things I have stored that I no longer use?

Mental: Which of my beliefs might be holding me back from a more abundant life? Am I holding any beliefs that are not mine?

Imagine what it would be like to set some of these belongings and beliefs free.

Release #1 (Belongings)

Walk through your house with an empty box. Fill it up with the first/obvious layer of things that don't make you feel expansive.

Give it away, one box at a time.

Repeat often.

Release #2 (Beliefs)

Our belief-clutter can be more difficult to find, which is why I like to start with the physical clearing and notice where my mind wants to hold on, and where it is ready to let go.

Did your first layer of physical clutter-clearing stir up any feelings of overwhelm or attachment, judgment or despair?

It might be a little early to blast these beliefs, so for now simply notice them, record any reflections in your simplicity journal, and move on to the next section.

If it felt completely energizing to start clearing and you have full belief that you are ready to let go of everything to live a more spacious and free life, you may not need this book...but I hope you will keep reading anyway.

Because most of the beliefs that will stop you will only show up when you go beneath the surface clutter and into the deeper crevices of your life.

The Deeper Questions

How will I know when what I have is enough?

Am I happy with how I'm using my resources? What is the trade-off between more stuff and more space?

Where is striving for more-better-different, impacting my sense of thriving NOW?

simply enough

Take 3 deep breaths.
You. Are. Essential.

Holding On

Fear of Not Enough

Have you lost your JOY
for the journey?

Perhaps you are hanging on too tight
to an old destination.

... or maybe you are carrying

way too much stuff.

When your world begins to overflow
in all the wrong places,

and life's clutter is crowding you,
creeping into your happiness,

it's time to make a choice:
stay buried beneath the excess

or release your hold
on whatever is holding onto you.

Pause. Loosen your grip.
It's time to let go.

And when you are no longer
holding so tight, clinging

to all you have been taught
you need, to succeed

you can finally rest
in the wide open spaces

where you are able
to fully receive.

A Story of Not Enough.

Have you heard the parable about a woman who has the opportunity to tour both heaven and hell?

The woman is first taken to hell, through the fiery gates and into a large room. What she sees is completely different than the images of hell she was taught as a child. There are tables and tables overflowing with food of every kind, goblets of golden wine, music, bounty everywhere. Yet the people sitting around the tables look famished and miserable. The woman is puzzled, but then she notices something strange.

The people in hell are holding long spoons, but their arms are unable to bend so it is impossible for them to feed themselves. So even though the people are sitting around tables laden with a generous supply of food, they are starving.

Interesting, she thinks, and asks to be taken to heaven. She walks through a different set of gates, these pearly, into another large room. Astonished, she sees exactly the same setting: tables overflowing with food, goblets of wine, music, people sitting around the tables with long spoons and unbending arms.

But in heaven, the people are smiling, laughing, dancing and glowing with good health.

There is one simple difference. In heaven, the people have learned to feed each other.

In hell, they are still holding on.

simply enough

Do you have any stories of 'not enough' in your life?

If so, when did those stories begin, and how are they influencing your relationship with your belongings, your ability to let go?

Maybe you can't pinpoint an exact beginning.

You may have grown up in a family where resources truly were limited and you learned from an early age to grab whatever you could get your hands on.

Or you were an only child, given everything you could have wished for, but at some point decided even *that* wasn't enough... or perhaps it was *too much* so you decided to renounce the material life and go live as a monk on a mountain top.

We all have stories of lack, abundance, and most everything in between.

The initial seeds of my story began in childhood, when I chose to believe there was not enough attention to go around. Those seeds grew as I bought into society's story that I had to work hard and compete, that success comes through accomplishment and striving to achieve.

My real story of lack and limitation didn't take root until later.

It came in a series of financial incidents that formed a belief that I needed to hang on tighter to the resources I had. Most of these situations were actually lessons in letting go, but I had to grasp tighter before I could release what was getting in the way of receiving something even greater.

Sometimes holding on too tight is like having unbending arms.

Contraction (and Courage to Expand)

I said earlier that I could barely imagine a life without plenty, and that is mostly true. But I *have* experienced loss, and I do know what it feels like to cling to something because I'm afraid of losing it.

My first lesson came after I left my corporate job to go into business with a man who pulled me onto my spiritual path, connected me with my most beloved teachers and friends, expanded my belief in possibility...then further activated my fear of not being or having enough.

When our partnership ended, I was left with a substantial debt, as well as an aching heart. A big dream was dying, and a part of my belief in myself was dying too. I felt like a failure.

I'd experienced frustration and disappointment before, but this time there was shame attached, so it left a crack in my trust in the world. Shame and failure are such heavy burdens, and it took years for me to even notice how much they had a hold on me.

I'll share more about how I let go of those stories later, but for now I have a more important story to tell.

This one begins when my daughter attempted to take her life. At the time, it was a total shock and completely knocked me off balance.

Of course it did. How could it not?

I was filled with a sense of guilt that my child, who seemed to have everything going for her, did not want to live. I felt I had somehow failed as a mother.

My heart broke, not only for my daughter, but also for myself...

for all the times I have wanted to turn off the pain of the world too. Fear came and my energy contracted. I didn't feel even close to enough.

This is a difficult story, and it is not completely mine to share. I asked my daughter's permission because I believe it is such an important part of this conversation about holding on.

We hold on when we are afraid of losing something we love. We hold on even tighter when we almost *do* lose that something. We carry burdens that are not meant to be carried alone.

Many are facing intense feelings of despair at the state of the world. It is so easy to give up, to turn to things that will numb the craziness, to shrink back from the pain or take it on as our own.

We are not meant to close our hearts to this intensity we feel. We are meant to open even more, to find compassion and the courage to show up fully for the world and the people right in front of us.

My daughter is on her own path, trying to navigate the complexities of the world. I trust her to find her way, and am so grateful she is still here sharing her love, creativity, humor, insight, and wisdom.

My part of this story is about holding on too tight, clinging to her happiness, sometimes at the expense of my own. It took years for me to see I was doing this. I still sometimes forget that I cannot live my children's lives for them, and they actually do much better when I give them space to find their own way.

But notice how even the *potential* of loss can impact our ability to let go, and how our experiences can cause us to hold on too tightly.

We don't have to hang onto the more painful experiences. We can let them help us expand in trust rather than contract through fear of loss.

Anais Nin wrote, *"Life shrinks or expands in proportion to one's courage."*

True courage is about moving through our fears to live in a more expansive state of love.

Don't let your stories have a hold on you.

Free them...and you will, in turn, be set free.

If you love something, set it free.
If it comes back, it's yours.
If it doesn't, you are both free.

Hanging On and Fear of Lack

It can be easy to understand why we hang on tight to what we love, but why do we hang on to the rest? Could it be that we fear not having enough?

I believe FEAR is the root of most every kind of clutter, from hoarding, to over-full closets and drawers, to impulse buying, over-eating, and difficulty being generous with what we have.

And this is nowhere more evident than when we look at our money. At some point in most lives, trust in having enough becomes tainted by doubt.

Maybe there really *isn't* enough to go around. Maybe I really *do* need to hold on and protect what I've worked so hard to gather. Obviously I need to fear loss because everywhere I turn, people are losing things.

So we hang on.

And because we are hanging on so tight to what we have managed to gather, the universal laws of FLOW begin to get distorted, then perhaps we really *don't* have enough. Or this is why there are others in the world who don't have enough.

The economic downturn of 2008 was the first massive reset that took the boomer generation by shock, causing many to lose homes, jobs, and big portions of their retirement portfolios. Years of slow but steady economic recovery and hard work have returned some of those losses.

But for others, my husband and I included, those losses started a series of resets that began paving the way to a different kind of security that doesn't come from our retirement accounts.

simply enough

We had to move through a lot of contraction and fear-based decision-making before we were ready to see that our freedom and security don't depend on how much money we have in the bank...because freedom and security are both a state of mind.

Finding the right balance between what we need to hold as part of a responsible financial foundation, and what we can allow to flow generously to support others, and ourselves, can be quite challenging. The balance point is different for everyone.

I sleep better and enjoy life more when I'm not worried about whether there is enough money in my account to pay bills this month. It also feels expansive to give money to causes I care about.

This is one reason my husband and I decided to restructure our lives to be mortgage and debt-free. It was not a simple decision, but that choice has helped us be more aligned with how we want to spend our lives: less tied to financial obligations, more free to give our time and money to what we love.

I have learned that as I ease my hold on what I have and am more generous with my giving, I receive everything I need.

I had a powerful experience of this after that first financial reset when we lost nearly half of our retirement savings. This is when I first started to understand the energy behind money and how it can limit our sense of enoughness.

Before I give you that story, take a few minutes to reflect on where you are hanging on too tightly, and how that might be limiting your experience of enough.

Reflect: What am I holding too tightly?

You've reflected on what you have gathered and the essence of what you want to keep. Now it's time to look at where you are holding on.

Consider each of the major areas of your life (home/work/ service/recreation/relationships/finances), asking yourself...

Which areas feel cluttered and messy, and which feel most light and spacious?

Where am I holding on most tightly, and where might it help to loosen my grip?

How is it serving me to keep holding on?

When we hold too tightly to what we have gathered, when we forget to share our bounty with others, the energy becomes stuck. Like the opening parable suggests, sharing can make the difference between heaven and hell.

simply enough

Which Comes First, Giving or Receiving?

But...it seems pretty obvious that you must have something before you can give it, right? So we gather, we hold on until we have enough, and then we can begin to share.

Well. Not necessarily.

Some of the least financially wealthy people I know are also the most generous. I have seen people with very small paychecks open their hearts and homes to feed the hungry and give the world clean water.

Giving isn't just about what you have in your bank account. It is a way of living that springs from generosity and a belief that we are here for one another. True generosity comes when we give from love and inspiration, not from obligation or a sense of duty.

When we learn to give from inspiration rather than obligation, there is receiving within the giving. There is no difference.

But, thoughts of generosity aside, what happens when we begin to give purely as an exercise in FLOW?

During that financial reset I mentioned earlier, we didn't have enough money coming in to cover our monthly expenses. I was in great anxiety over finances and had stopped most of our monthly donations because I believed there was not enough. My normal positive outlook was replaced by fear, worry, and resentment.

I began holding on very tightly to what we still had.

Then, one night an angel came to me in a dream. She floated down until she was right in front of me, looked me in the eye and said, *"Give of your money."*

I woke the next morning with a resolve to follow that advice. I re-instated a couple of monthly donations, wrote a few random generosity checks, and smiled at how good it felt to be giving again. Within a week, two properties that were draining our cash flow sold, and we received an unexpected check in the mail.

It was such an immediate response that I knew it was an important message for me to remember and to share: open to greater financial flow through giving.

It is so easy to be in fear with our finances, one of the most basic forms of security. Somehow, the simple act of giving even a few dollars says, "I know this is important and I am going to believe there is more where this came from."

So if you are waiting to receive more time, more energy, more money, more *anything* before you give, don't wait any longer. Find something that inspires you and just start giving.

When you give from a place of inspiration, you will receive all you need to keep the flow going.

simply enough

A Simple Lesson in Energy Flow

If you are not quite convinced, here is an activity I used to do after another dream and angel message inspired me to launch *The Everyday Miracle Network* in 2010. It was an attempt to help myself and others appreciate the concept of giving and receiving as interconnected flow, at the same time we created grassroots impact in our community.

This was also one of my first forays into the power of collaborative giving, which reinforced my understanding that when we open our channel of giving wider, more flows through.

Imagine this.

You are sitting in a large circle of people, with everyone holding a single dollar bill. A chime rings and you are instructed to turn to the left to hand the dollar to the person sitting there. But since everyone is turning to the left, there is nobody to receive your dollar. You are left holding the money you are trying to give.

Lesson #1: Without receiving, there can be no giving.

You get the idea and open your right hand to receive, but then get so focused on receiving that you forget to give to the person on your left...and it doesn't take long before you end up with a pile of money while others in the circle have none.

Lesson #2: Without giving, there is an interruption in the flow of receiving.

In a perfect world, the flow of giving and receiving continues in perfect balance, everyone receiving what they need and nobody left without.

Now consider what might happen if the single dollar is replaced with a $1000 bill. Will it be easier to give to the person sitting on your left, especially if you are not confident in the one on your right?

Same exercise, but how often is our ability to give (and receive) money interrupted by the number of zeros attached?

Lesson #3: To open your flow of receiving, you must open your channel of giving.

This is an extreme over-simplification of how energy works, but it is a powerful reminder that we need to have BOTH giving and receiving to keep the FLOW going.

And while this is a powerful way to demonstrate how the energy of money is meant to stay in motion, it works for other things equally well.

As the saying goes, "give what you want to receive." Which takes practice.

simply enough

Practice: Open to Flow

That simple exercise powerfully demonstrates the concept of FLOW, but it takes great faith to actually put the idea into practice. For most of us, there is a natural tendency to hold on when we are not sure we will have enough.

So how do we start opening our flow of giving when we are in a place of lack? We start with opening space.

Reflect

Physical: Look at where the clutter in your home spaces might be blocking energy flow.

Do you have to search through your closets and drawers to find what you need?

Is there space to work on your desk and counters?

Look closely to see what might be interrupting your flow as well as taking up space. Clutter steals both time and energy from what you love.

Mental: Consider what is getting in the way of clearing those piles.

What habits would you have to change to open some of those spaces?

Could any of your clutter be put to better use?

Open your mind to the spaciousness it will feel when the clutter is gone. Open your heart to the love it will feel when your resources are put to use.

Release

Try some of these Simple Energy Practices for Opening Flow.

Surface clearing: Clear everything that doesn't have a use from your floors, counters, and other surfaces. Put it all in a box, out of sight. Notice if the energy feels different in your home or office without the surface clutter.

Mental clearing: Scan your body, noticing where you might be storing any tension, stress, worry, concern, or fear around what you are holding. Breathe in and let the emotion move through. *Now go get a massage!*

Schedule clearing: Remove everything from your schedule that doesn't feel joyful or expansive. Now add some empty space in between each commitment. Fill those spaces with silence and some deep breaths of being.

Financial clearing: If your money feels limited, consider giving a small donation to something or someone that inspires you. Trust there will be more.

Technology clearing: There are so many layers here, so let's start on the surface.

> *Email: Clear your inbox! Delete and repeat. If it doesn't go into a "save folder" of the most important things that you really need to save, get rid of it. You won't have time to read it later. Trust me.*

simply enough

Computer: Empty your desktop of all the programs and documents you don't regularly access. Create folders to hold the rest.

Phone: Offload all the excess APPS. Turn off notifications unless you really need them.

Now, resolve to take at least one tech-free day every week. Spend time in nature. Nurture your relationships. Your messages will wait for you.

Bonus Practice: Open your Giving Flow

If you have any areas in your life that are stagnant or depleted, try giving more of whatever is feeling stuck. Here are a few ideas.

Give-a-Dollar-a-Day: This is a magical way to experience how consistently giving a small amount of money can open more than monetary flow. Gather 30 one-dollar bills at the start of each month, then carry them with you and find creative ways to give away one dollar, every day. (Leave one in a library book, on someone's windshield, in a napkin holder...) Do this for a month to see what happens. Even if your money flow doesn't increase, you'll have fun thinking of creative ways to leave a gift!

Give a Treasure a Day: This is a fun way to clear physical clutter. The intention is to challenge yourself by giving things you truly treasure, stretching to give where you might still have some level of attachment. It doesn't have to be a physical treasure, but that is an excellent way to move your possessions.

Join a Giving Circle: There are a number of collaborative giving groups that gather small donations to create bigger impact. I have links to a few of these on my website. Join an existing group or create your own!

Whatever you give, notice how your flow of receiving is impacted. Pay attention to where your treasure lies, and be willing to share it abundantly with others.

The Deeper Questions

What am I holding onto that is no longer serving (my relationships, my spiritual evolution, my sense of peace, my happiness)?

Am I holding onto anything that is keeping me from what is most essential?

simply enough

Ahhhhh.

3 more deep breaths.

What is most essential...now?

Letting Go

Enough is Enough!

When your pack gets too heavy...
loosen your grip, lighten your load.

It's time to Let Go.

In the end, does it really matter

that you filled your days

with anything but more space

for what (and whom) you love?

What might life give you
if you let go, fully, and simply o p e n
to the gifts that are already here?

When life gets too full,
it's easy to miss what matters.

Empty
to be full of what does.

Reflections on Letting Go

I used to think letting go was something you did when your closet and drawers got too full, or perhaps when something had become too small or confining, as with a relationship or job.

Then letting go was what I had to do to stay sane as a full-time mother with a career. Even though I was pretty awesome at both, there is only so much super-woman can do to change the world while being a super-mom.

At some point, letting go became the spiritual thing to do... quiet the ego, be more heart-centered, return to the essential, live in connection with nature and God. Forgive the past. Live in the present.

Ommmm.

I hope you are laughing, as laughter is one of the absolute best ways to move from holding on to letting go.

Because, let's face it: letting go is one of the most important things we can learn. In the end, there is really nothing else to do.

One of my letting go stories began when I enrolled in a 30 day 'Passion Project' for my business. The very first day, I realized my 'project' was going to be to release all my projects so I could reconnect with something that had gone missing from my life.

I was exhausted, and the last thing I needed was another project. With tears flowing, I wrote to the group leader and told her what I planned to do.

While others were busy creating new juicy programs for their clients, I got busy Creating Space: letting go of all that was distracting me from living in alignment with my inner JOY.

simply enough

I started by creating more space in my work-life, letting go of incomplete projects and expectations of what my business was *supposed* to look like to be considered successful. I cleared everything from my calendar for 30 days, telling my clients I was taking a simplification sabbatical.

That sabbatical lasted a lot longer than a month. It became a way of life.

I now make ongoing choices to clear surface clutter in order to stay engaged with what is most meaningful and joyful, and this feels like a perpetual vacation to me.

So, while it was intended to jump start a single project that would help revitalize my business, the 30 day Passion Project ended up showing me all the ways I was covering the essence of what was most important in my life.

It gave permission to follow a different path and trust that even in the letting go, perhaps especially in the letting go, is where true meaning can be found.

Notice that the very first place I began to clear space was my calendar. When we are so overly 'busy' with obligations, appointments, gatherings, and endless things to DO, there is no way we can begin to find the inner spaciousness, much less make time to clear our outer clutter.

So consider which of your obligations, appointments, and commitments are really feeding your soul right now. Maybe you have outgrown that book club and would rather spend more time in your garden. Perhaps your child would benefit more from having time in the garden just being with you, rather than going to another lesson or sports activity.

So much of life and love is about holding on. We spend our lives attaching to things we love: family, friends, partners, ideas, art, projects, and possessions. But what if the only reason we are attaching and creating is for the ultimate life lesson that will bring something even better?

What if the only way to experience this ultimate life lesson is to LET GO of everything we think we love, so we can open more completely to the simple joy of being?

Life is made of thousands of moments, and when we are so busy striving and chasing our dreams, it's easy to miss the essence of those moments.

Perhaps it's time to slow down, savor the stillness, let go of what we are hanging onto so tightly and simply open our hearts wide to what is already here.

simply enough

Letting go is not just about releasing
what is no longer meaningful.

It's a state of mind and heart,
an inner cloak of simplicity
that shields us as we move through
the chaos of everyday living.

Letting go is releasing both past and future
to embrace the present moment
as the Gift it is meant to be.

When enough becomes too much.

Baskets of apples. Fields of flowers. Rooms of people.

It is easy to visualize what happens when we gather too much. Rotten fruit. Wilting flowers. Unhappy people.

So how do we know when to stop gathering?

Most of us have a natural ability to know what is too much when it comes to food and perishable items. Why then, do we have over-full closets and drawers, garages and storage units, pantry shelves and utensil drawers, calendars and minds.

When did it become fashionable to keep more than we need or use, and to wear busyness like a badge of honor?

Perhaps when life began to stuff more into our calendars and brains, when we began finding less time and space to connect with the simpler joys of life. As you begin yearning for more of this time and space, you may also begin wondering if you really need all those physical belongings.

Not everyone goes through a simplification phase of letting go of physical belongings. Some people remain happy with their accumulated possessions their entire life. Then they die and leave their house-full of clutter to their children. (grin)

If you don't want to be one of those people, and I am quite sure you don't if you are reading this book, then it's time to get busy letting go of some of the layers.

But first, let's go on a little vacation. Traveling always makes me re-consider how much of my stuff I really need.

simply enough

Lighten Your Load

Whenever I travel, I come back with renewed commitment for a simpler life. For one thing, packing what I need for a couple of weeks or even a month reminds me how much I do *not* need. Almost always, I pack way more than enough for my journey, even when I focus on traveling lightly.

I want to be prepared for everything, so I bring more than the bare essentials.

The same goes for my home. I like to be prepared for company, for changes of weather, for impending inspiration that is sure to take me back to my paints and boxes of collage materials some day. I love knowing I have extra food in my pantry and freezer. I like walking through my home feeling both spacious and abundant. My home is organized, but not minimalized.

I love having a prosperous life.

But there is a more important reason I feel called to simplicity after traveling, especially when I venture outside of the United States. I see how happy the people are in the countries where simple is a way of life, and I feel how happy *I am* when I connect to that simple life...a life of just enough that feels so very abundant.

In the United States, it is more popular to have excess than to want for anything, and many of us have been taught to continue wanting more, even when we already have everything we need.

It's not our fault that the pursuit of the American dream got ingrained, or that our competitive society keeps urging us to reach higher, to keep striving for a more abundant life. Our potential is at stake. And we don't want to be lazy and unproductive. That's what leads to poverty and homelessness, isn't it?

Sigh. It sounds so obviously wrong to write that, and I absolutely do not believe that sentence about poverty, but it is a belief system that I know is ingrained in parts of our American culture. I admit, there is something in my genes that feels lazy if I don't happen to want to keep striving for more.

Even after we have begun to seek meaning and fulfillment more than success, and we are at a place in life of not having to worry about the bare essentials, it can be a challenge to shift from gathering to simply enjoying what we have. The laws of gravity and motion work on many levels, and it is not easy to stop accumulating when so much of life is focused on gathering.

I will repeat what I said in the introduction, because I know many are struggling with this same conundrum.

There is nothing wrong with gathering, or even with having more than enough.

But when those layers of accumulated belongings and beliefs begin to get in the way of our happiness, productivity, relationships, and fulfillment...it's time to let go.

This does NOT mean we have to give up our belongings, but that they no longer rule us by taking so much energy to keep.

simply enough

Reflect: What am I ready to release?

Before you do any heavy lifting, consider these questions. Otherwise, you may end up moving piles from the house to the garage and not actually getting rid of anything. (Not that I've ever done that, but I think my husband has. ;-)

Where is my stuff getting in the way of my efficiency and productivity?

What am I holding onto that might be of use to someone else?

How might more spaciousness in (name an area) create more freedom?

When you begin to get clear on what you no longer need, and what may be getting in the way of your happiness, it is likely because you are beginning to see beyond your own life into a more conscious way of living in the world.

You may have a call toward a specific cause that grows more important than having another outfit hanging in your closet or set of dishes to replace the perfectly good ones you just gave away.

Like me, you may feel the heart of the world breaking and know there is more to do than create organized and simple spaces.

However the call comes, I hope you will have space in your life to answer.

A Call to Simplify

My call to simplicity came through a series of mid-life awakenings. Yours is likely the same, unless you have had one of those sudden wake-up calls that feels disastrous at the time then turns into a blessing in disguise.

For most of us, there is a gradual opening of our awareness to see the world from a wider perspective, not quite so caught up in the more self-invested energy we need while we are still forming our identity and building our life's foundation.

When I started to become less focused on my personal and family needs, I didn't know where to even begin.

How do I reconcile the naked fact that there are people in this world with few possessions, difficult access to food and clean water, while here I am with more belongings than I could ever possibly use?

I don't.

There IS no reconciling, because there is no balance sheet when it comes to life, and what I am still learning is that there can be no comparison either. No comparison.

We each have unique lessons to learn, gifts to share, and realizations to teach with our one precious life. I know this, so why do I continue to feel uneasy with the disparity that indeed exists around the world?

Perhaps because this is my personal call to serve, and as I continue to get rid of what I no longer need, I always find new ways to answer that call.

So whether I am giving away material possessions, raising money to give clean water, helping a neighbor, or advocating for some kind of systemic change that will impact many, I have come to believe that whatever I am called to do is *exactly* enough.

Your call will be different, even if you resonate with mine. If you don't already know what is calling you, look for it beneath your life's clutter.

This is at least part of what clearing clutter is for...to open space that can be filled with more meaning.

And when the problems of the world still feel overwhelming and we don't know what we can possibly do to answer the call, it is time to empty even more.

What is asked of us,
over and over and over, is to empty.
To offer our empty hands.
To let the things we are holding so
tightly just drop.
To give it all up, everything,
that does not exist in this moment.
Everything that has happened,
that we think we somehow need to do
something about,
everything we think might happen, or
we hope will happen,
every sweet dream that we cling to.
This is God's loving strip search.
Give it all over.
Something else wants to live you.
And you can feel it.

–Jeannie Zandi

Empty

Letting go is the heart of enough, and it is the part of this book that actually stalled me out for quite a while. I have been writing about letting go for years, but as I peered into the layers that I have explored with my writing and my life...well, it felt like something was missing.

My brain kept looking for some secret formula that would at some point keep the clutter from creeping back to encroach upon my happiness with its constant messiness.

And now I know what I was missing: life IS messy, and letting go is an art.

Letting go has less to do with getting rid of material possessions, and more to do with the ART of knowing how to EMPTY.

I smile when I think of all the hours I have spent moving physical clutter around while trying to find some sense of inner order. Clearing clutter on the outside is one of the ways I clear my mind and move my emotions. Organizing is part of my personal art of letting go, and my husband knows to leave me alone if I have a sudden drive to clean out every closet in the house.

Moving through the outer layers of clutter is one of the ways I return to empty, or at least put a bit of space around whatever is crowding my inner peace.

But what would it feel like to STAY empty?

We will likely never know, because life keeps filling us up, and no matter how hard we try to clear it, the clutter always comes back.

    Mental clutter: thoughts, judgments, full calendars.

Emotional clutter: hurts and heartaches, attachments and heartbreaks, worry.

Physical clutter: incoming mail, laundry, dirty dishes, changing styles.

To live as an empty vessel takes much attention and commitment. Every morning, we clear the obvious clutter and begin again.

My morning ritual is essential and I am very cranky without it.

It begins with sitting in spacious thought, simply listening. Whether to the the song of my soul, the sound of birdsong, raindrops, or the stillness of a sunrise, I invite my senses to awaken gently before they are bombarded with the more abrasive noises of life.

Next I participate in a daily spiritual teaching that inspires me to aspire to even more spaciousness. Finally, I begin to move my body around the house, doing some light stretching at the same time I clear surface clutter, empty the dishwasher, water plants, and whatever else my home needs to feel spacious and organized.

While I move, I also give thanks. When I make time for this practice, I feel more positive in general, as well as more prepared to face any challenges that might come.

In her book, "365 Ways to Live Generously," Sharon Lipinski calls this practice: Meditate. Motivate. Move. This is a good way to engage spirit/mind/body as we begin another day of loving.

And this is the bigger reason we empty...to give more space to what we love, and to be more *full* of love, too.

As a highly sensitive person (HSP), I need to empty more often than most. My nervous system requires it, and helps me by going into overload if I neglect to clear out the excess on a regular basis. So I have cultivated a system of clearing habits, cleanses, and simplification sabbaticals to keep my inner-HSP happy.

I will share more about these practices in the flow section, since they were initially the reason I decided to write this book. Then something interesting happened when I started to go deeper with my own journey to simple.

I opened so much space in my life, cleared out so many layers of clutter, and dropped so many perceived commitments that I was ready for something more. I discovered that beneath everything, there was a desire to give my life more fully to something Greater. I was ready to be guided differently, and it required a lot of open space and letting go to be even close to ready for that kind of divine intervention.

This is the ultimate letting go, releasing attachments not only to physical possessions, but also to self-inflicted ideas and thoughts, plans and goals. Spacious living is being open to inner guidance rather than following some prescribed notions of what you *should* do. (This is *your* journey, afterall.)

We learn the delicate art of letting go, not by following simplification check-lists and joining on-line clutter-clearing challenges, but through the slow process of cultivating spaciousness, inside and out.

And that will take practice.

Practice: Get Comfortable with Empty

To many, the word empty brings images of lack. To me, it means spacious possibility.

When a cup is empty, it is open to receive fresh liquid. When a page is empty, it is open to receive fresh words, a new story that has never been told.

When a mind is empty, it has room to listen. When a heart is empty, it has room to receive.

When your day is empty of have-to-do's, there is plenty of space for anything you want to do.

To open completely to anything new, you must first be empty of everything old.

Let yourself get comfortable with empty.

simply enough

Reflect:

Consider where more space might offer you more time, energy, peace of mind, or happiness.

Physical: Notice how FULL the various areas of your physical space are (house, garage, office, car, yard, storage unit).

Are there any areas that might be more beautiful, efficient, welcoming if they were a tiny bit more empty?

Mental: Now look at your calendar and computer.

Are you giving yourself enough open space in between meetings, events, and commitments to be open to possibility? Is your inbox overflowing? Is any other computer clutter distracting you?

Emotional: Finally, take a moment to consider your inner space.

Do you have any toxic relationships or emotions (such as resentment, anger, disappointment) you are hanging onto that could free up space for more love/compassion/understanding?

Release:

Now is the time to begin the process of releasing some of the layers. This is an ongoing process, so don't expect to do it in a single sweep.

However, if you have gotten clear with the first sections of this book, you will make a bigger impact and your clearing will be more lasting.

Make time to empty, every day, as often as you can. It will keep you clear and more available to attend to whatever it is you are called to do.

Clear clutter from your counters, floors, sinks at least once every week, if not every single day.

Quiet the waves of thought from your mind between every activity during your day. Sit in silence, move to some gentle music, stand on the earth, take a few deep breaths of being in between your busy doing.

Create intentional space in your calendar to simplify and return to essence. You will be amazed at how much more present and productive you will be.

Clear your computer inbox at least weekly, and take one day each week to be completely tech free. This simple practice will free more than just your time.

Treat your relationships as if you are seeing each person for a last time. Stay complete and empty of toxicity with your relationships, and you will be free.

What other ways can you think of to add S P A C E to your life?

The Deeper Questions

Are any of my beliefs getting in the way of my ability to let go?

What makes it easy or difficult for me to let go?

How might my letting go serve others?

simply enough

Simple Tips for Letting Go

I use these practices personally as well as with mentoring clients. While they may seem simple on the surface, they are powerful techniques for staying clear and shining.

Feel It Fully. To fully embrace life, we must experience the full range of our feelings before moving into each new experience. Denying, ignoring, repressing, minimizing our feelings can add layers of emotional burden.

Complete. Living with completion is a mindful practice that allows every experience to be simply what it is, for now, so that we can move on without pieces of our attention left behind. It invites us to live more fully in the present moment by saying (aloud or to yourself), "I am Complete" before moving on.

See the Silver Lining. Each new challenge is an opportunity: the silver lining. What may appear as a 'crisis' is most always a matter of perception. When you feel challenged, ask "Where is the silver lining?" The more you practice, the faster you will find the light beaming from behind the clouds.

Next... This powerful word can unleash incredible energy to get you unstuck. It creates an opening in the mind to release what no longer serves you, opening the mind to new thoughts and choices. To accelerate the shift, use the breathing technique, described...next!

Breathe 5*5*5. Breathing is one of the fastest ways to move energy. Try this 5*5*5 breathing technique. Simply inhale slowly and evenly for 5 counts, hold for 5 counts, then exhale for 5 counts. Do this five times. Once you have the rhythm, add a smile as you breathe.

Laugh! Laughter is a cure for just about everything. It will help you forgive your mistakes, or at least take them more lightly. Laughter energizes and keeps us in touch with our child-like nature. Find the humor in any situation by thinking of yourself as a child looking in wonder and amusement at the silliness of serious adults.

1-2-3 Shine. Let go of the everyday stress that lands in the body by nourishing body, mind, and spirit. Give your body adequate rest, nourishment and exercise. Keep your mind positive through loving relationships, a conscious support group, active service. Polish your spirit with meditation, prayer, affirmations, inspirational readings or audio programs.

And remember: if you are in the middle of a letting go challenge on the mental or emotional level, try cleaning out one of your physical clutter areas. It's amazing how much perspective you can gain from organizing even a single messy drawer or closet.

Now, let go of letting go.

Rest in what you love.

Abundance

More than Enough

Do you still love where you're going?

(Try loving where you are.)

We begin with nothing.
And, in that nothing, we are enough.

We grow. We learn to attach.
We separate from enough.

The layers accumulate:
emotional: was I loved enough?
physical: do I have enough?
spiritual: am I giving enough?

We acquire. We learn to want.
We believe there is security in having.

We cover the essence with more.
We yearn to be seen, to be full
so we gather even more.

We strive to be successful
so we reach higher, for still more.

More. More. More.

Until one day
it is time to begin again.

To begin to look
through a different lens,
To begin to see
with uncluttered eyes,
To begin to feel
with a wide-open heart,
Into the space
where everything flows.

No possession. No attachment.
Empty and Full.
All One.

More than Enough.

Simple Abundance

The gathering has stopped. The sorting has happened. We have opened our hands and our hearts to let go of what we have been holding so tight.

And now there is so much S P A C E.

What will we fill it with?

How do we allow abundance and empty to exist simultaneously?

When we have plenty, and we still yearn for more, perhaps there will never be enough.

When we open space, then fill it up again, perhaps there is a deeper emptiness still waiting to be filled that has nothing to do with our physical belongings.

As I look around the room where I sit writing about abundance, I see more than just plenty of possessions. I see beauty. I see memories.

I love my belongings, yet I know that I no longer belong to them.

They are a part of my life, but I would walk away from them if I decided they were keeping me too small.

At least I think I could.

But this is the life I created, and for now it is enough to be grateful for what I keep while being careful to not be possessed by what I own.

Outside the window across from my writing desk, a few trees are still covered in leaves, while others stand bare and beautiful against a clear blue sky.

simply enough

Nature never hangs on to what it no longer needs.

Or does it? There are clusters of grapes still clinging to the vines after the frost has turned all the leaves brown and shriveled. I wonder how long they will hang on before they finally decide it is time to let go.

I turn to nature to simplify, but nature is actually quite complex.

Perhaps the essence of simple abundance is what we find in nature: a constant movement of creating, letting go, growing, giving.

Perhaps what we are looking for when we are ready to let go of so many external possessions is simply a willingness to be in this state of perpetual giving.

Those grapes that clung to the vines became a winter offering for birds that virtually flocked around the bare branches. They were grateful for the hanging on and were ready to receive when the vines were finally ready to let go.

Where in your life might you release some of your abundance to fill another's need?

Let your space fill up again, if that makes you happy—just keep pruning the over-growth and sharing your harvest.

This is the only way abundance will keep growing for you.

More than enough.

I could never write or say or do anything to help you know how much you will have when you finally let go of all the layers of excess you have accumulated. Nothing anyone can teach will get you to the ultimate place of abundance, where you have everything you could want, and would give it all away in a moment, upon the asking, if that was what was needed.

The peace/love/fulfillment you are searching for is hard to find when you go looking for it. While you may find what you seek for a moment, those feelings will only last when something takes root deep within your Soul that knows *this is more than enough.* And you can only find this knowing through surrender to what you already have. It is nothing outside of you.

You might not believe in 'God' in the traditional way. You may connect instead with nature or music or art, feeling a majesty that goes beyond words to a spacious emptiness that is full of unseen vibrancy.

However you experience life's mystery, the expansiveness of unbound love, this is where you will find your *more.*

Some people read the bible or other spiritual texts to find that mystery, or to know what they are supposed to believe. Perhaps some will find the source of their faith there, but can we ever truly know divine Love from reading a book?

I was raised Catholic and cannot actually remember reading the bible. I went through confirmation and received communion and felt reverence when I put on my hat and lace gloves and pretty dress for Easter service. Maybe I felt the seeds of something in those early days, but the expansive Love I now know as God came much later.

simply enough

It came after I let go of the belief in a God outside of me.

One of my friends has experienced years of physical challenge, and some days she wonders why she is still here. As we were sitting on the patio one day, she began talking of her spiritual connection. She was surrounded by peace as she connected with that divine Presence she knows as God.

We all have different ways to describe our experience of the divine. None are more right, because they all come through a unique way of perceiving the world.

But when my friend turned around and told me she doesn't know what love is because she was abused as a child and never really loved by her parents, I asked her to go back to that experience of holy Presence she had just described to me.

What did that feel like? What would she name that?

Most of us will never experience the full expanse of Love we call God/Spirit/Oneness from any relationship we might have on earth. It is rare for a relationship to hold the kind of unconditional Love that exists when you open beyond the physical form to the unfathomable mystery of life.

But it is here, and you will feel it when you make time to clear your life enough to live in connection with that mystery.

Where do YOU connect to YOUR *more-than-enough*?

Does it come when you walk through a forest or beside an ocean or through a field of wildflowers or up to the very top of the highest mountain you can find...and you feel both vast and small as you embrace the majesty?

Do you feel it when you gaze out to a vast horizon and feel your energy expand to the far reaches of what your eyes are seeing, or when you meet the gaze of a baby and feel your heart melt into her eyes?

Do you feel *more-than-enough* when you sit still, or as you dance with abandon around your living room, by yourself or in the arms of a lover?

Do you know *more-than-enough* when your eyes are closed, as you listen to an inner song, or as you turn up the volume of your favorite holy music?

However you experience a connection to YOUR *more-than-enough*, let that be what guides you to live in a state of abundance where you are holding onto nothing, while knowing you have everything.

This is the way to true and lasting abundance.

And when you find your place of abundance, don't hold too tight or it might break you. I learned this lesson from my plum tree.

simply enough

Plum Abundance: A Story of Over-Giving

Sometimes even nature doesn't know when enough is enough.

The branches were bowing low, and I knew it was nearing time to pluck the ripening fruit. We pruned and pruned earlier in the spring, but you would never know it from the hundreds of small round cherry-plums hanging heavy from our tree.

Then one day, it was too late. The branches grew too heavy. Perhaps the tree was weakened when last year's snowstorm claimed one of her main branches. Maybe our pruning was wrong or not enough. For whatever reason, the branches broke and I came home to that minor disaster.

We trimmed with love and a prayer that the tree would find strength again to keep offering her shade to our front porch. Then we set to work collecting as much of the fruit as we could from the broken branches.

Buckets and buckets of fruit. Gallons and gallons of plum juice. Some canned to save for another season. Some offered freely to neighbors.

There were times during the gathering and sorting and condensing of this labor of plum rescue that I lost patience. But when I stayed present to the simple joy of clearing one branch at a time, preparing one batch at a time, then joyfully sharing the fruits of our labor, there was a ripening of my own understanding as well.

When enough becomes too much, it can burden or break us.

The story of the plums is not so different from any other story of gathering, sorting, clearing layers of excess to get to the essence. The plums just make it more necessary to do it NOW, because if you wait too long, all you will have is rotten fruit.

Our plum tree definitely over-produced, and the result was more than just broken branches. It was a reminder to pay attention to excess, to trim back where needed, to harvest what we can, and to share our abundance with others.

I'm glad I was listening.

Are there any over-abundant, over-giving, over-producing areas in your life?

(Don't let them break you!)

simply enough

Reflect: Where do I have more than enough?

You likely still have layers of letting go possibility and are not done clearing your clutter yet. You never will be. I am taking you beneath the surface clutter with this book, but there will always be surface clutter to deal with.

And until you know what it means to feel 'abundant' even *without* any external stuff, you will continue to gather more than you need.

So take time to consider...

What does abundance look and feel like to me?

Where do I already have enough, and more than enough, in my life?

Do I have any areas of over-gathering (or giving) that are breaking my natural flow?

When you make time to notice and appreciate your abundance, it will be easier to let go of what you really don't need.

Make time—often—to reflect on where your life feels abundant.

Be grateful for what you have, and you will continue to have more than enough.

How to say Thank You (and mean it).

Close your eyes...or open them wide.
Bow your head...or raise your eyes to heaven.

With hands on heart, smile.
Say Thank You.

Breathe the words into your core.
Thank You.

Beam the words into the world.
Thank You.

Say the words again and again.
Thank You. Thank You. Thank You.

What can be more simple than this?
Every way...Every day,
Give Thanks.

From Overwhelm to Overflow

Abundance, by definition, means a large amount, affluence, fullness. But when we are already full and we reach for MORE without making time to even notice what we are holding, abundance can turn to greed.

How do we keep our abundance from becoming an insatiable hunger, where we are always striving to be-do-have something more?

We give thanks.

Authentic gratitude helps fullness overflow, creating an outpouring of loving that embraces the moment, whatever it holds. I added the word *authentic* because thanks can become an automated response, something you learn to say out of politeness or habit.

When we give thanks from deep within our core, gratitude grows. It wraps around all parts of life and keeps abundance flowing.

Authentic gratitude is a deep reverence for what you are beholding, whether that be someone you love, something you have, or the simple beauty and blessing of whatever life is giving you in the moment.

I like to call this, great fullness, because it reminds me to keep noticing and filling up with what is great about my life, until the blessings naturally overflow.

How do we stay in this perpetual state of gratitude overflow?

We become empty of expectation, full of wonder. We move at the pace of joy, opening our eyes wide, our hearts wider, making time to see beauty and celebrate the good in the world.

But what about all the bad things happening in the world?

As we witness the beyond-awful circumstances around the world, while living a life of ease and grace and so much abundance, it can feel wrong to stay grateful. I have experienced anger, disappointment, and depression over the disparity, but when I get stuck in these emotions, they are just more clutter.

When I listen to my heart telling me to be grateful for the life I have and to never take it for granted, I am more able to pay attention to where my emotions are directing me to focus in a different way.

Gratitude for our own blessings can turn anger, despair, and disappointment into compassionate action, where we are able to overflow our blessings to others.

So clear some of the busyness from your life, the fullness from your calendar, the over-abundance from your living spaces, and let your gratitude (and your blessings) flow.

simply enough

Be like the blazing maple tree in fall,

giving everything

in one colorful blast of amazement

...then dropping everything

to stand naked

against an expansive blue sky.

Grow a Legacy of Love

As we connect to our inner abundance and let our blessings flow, life becomes more than an accumulation of material wealth. It takes on a deeper, richer texture that is full of meaning and fulfillment. You don't need material possessions to have that sense of abundance. You don't need material wealth to create a lasting legacy.

Your life is your legacy, not your wealth.

When you understand this, whatever you choose to keep in your outer world, you are ready to live without being overly attached to it. This is the final phase in the journey to a more simple life: freedom to live in a perpetual flow of generosity.

When we are less attached to our physical belongings and an overly full calendar, we are free to show up more generously in life. This is what we will be remembered by, not the great feats we accomplished, the collections we gathered, or the size of our bank accounts.

We will be remembered by how well we loved.

So whether you are pursuing a big dream, creating beautiful art, delivering clean water, growing gardens, designing a community gathering place, writing a book, feeding the homeless, loving a child, taking care of aging parents, or leading a civil rights movement...remember that you are building a legacy by being fully present and real in all the simple ways you show up, day after day.

True and lasting abundance comes through practicing loving, and being grateful for, the ones we are with.

Practice: Gratitude + Generosity = Grace

When you are in touch with your inner abundance...when you know that nothing you have on the outside could possibly equal what you have inside of you...when you are FULL of wonder and EMPTY of need...it is time to exercise your gratitude, expand your generosity, and open to grace.

Exercise Your Gratitude

Gratitude is a muscle that needs to be stretched regularly, but not through some forced routine. If you keep a gratitude journal or list, make sure you are connecting with the heart of what you write about. Take a few minutes to breathe gratitude into your heart before you write.

Then share your gratitude out loud. This is the way to fully exercise your gratitude muscle, not by keeping it all to yourself.

My favorite prolific artist-muse, Brian Andreas (flyingedna.com), suggests 'Five Easy Steps' to get your gratitude glowing.

1. *Pick someone you know.*
2. *Stop everything you're doing and really look at them.*
3. *Tell them why they make your heart melt. Try to use actual concrete examples, sort of like this:*

I love the way your whole face lights up when something makes you laugh unexpectedly...or how you get about ten feet tall and lightning sparks around your hair when someone isn't treated with love and care and respect...or that way you come over and sit beside me and hold my hand and say, this is my favorite part.

4. Give them a hug and send them back into the world.

Pick someone else. Do all of this again with them.

5. Later, after a day that glows more than usual, wonder why you don't do this more often.

Expand Your Generosity

Give what you want to receive.

Consider where generosity might create even more abundance in your life, then ask yourself...

How can I get more creative with my generosity?

Are there any ways I might be more generous with my friends/family/neighbors?

Are there any ways I need to be more generous with myself?

Generosity is more about *how* we give than what we are actually giving.

Give without expectation, from a place of connection, and with no attachment to how the giving will be received.

Give a smile to a stranger, a love letter to a friend, a jar of fresh grape juice to a neighbor, a donation to build a school across the world, an email that may touch someone's heart in just the right way today.

Then give yourself time and space to do something you love. Like most everything, the flow of generosity must begin within.

Experience Grace

As you commit to practicing new ways to exercise your gratitude and expand your generosity, you will notice your life beginning to be blessed in ways you hadn't expected.

Give this practice a try for 21 days and notice where your life feels more full of grace, ease and flow, a bit more empty of stress.

The Deeper Questions

How might my abundance serve others?

How do I stay connected to the energy of abundance, no matter what is happening around me?

What is the legacy I want to create with my life?

Here, in the small moments of life, is
where your true legacy finds you.

Not grown of material wealth,
possessions passed along,
monuments built or dreams fulfilled.

Your legacy is shaped
in a thousand simple moments of giving.

A smile that springs from your heart,
a song that has to be sung,
a trust given, a hand reached out.

Single beads of kindness strung together
to grow a generous life.

Your legacy is not a destination,
but an everyday journey to give
what your Soul knows is yours to give.

It is written in the hearts
of every life you touch.

Touch with care and compassion.
Grow a legacy of love.

Flow

Simply Enough

When you love where you are,

you are ready to...

Simply. Be. Love.

When life's layers
and overflowing closets
are no longer crowding you...

When you are willing to let go
of all you no longer need
to get where you are ready to go...

When life's abundance
is where you go to fill up,
not something you want to buy...

You are finally free.

No longer captive,
only captivated
by life's ongoing mystery.

Learning to Flow

Even when you find your place of simple abundance, living gratefully and generously within the size of life that is just right for you...something is bound to change.

Life will constantly move between not-enough and more-than enough.

So how do we stay in a flow state, where everything moves in a free and fluid stream, nothing blocking our progress or happiness?

You probably know my answer by now. We don't.

We can learn to move around the blocks and climb over the barriers, but being in flow isn't about removing all the obstacles. There will always be obstacles, just like the clutter will always come back if you let it. Life will never come at you in a perfect, manageable flow.

It is YOU who needs to learn to flow with life.

Sure, you may still want to have goals and dreams. (Until you are ready to open to an even more adventurous way of living without them.)

But, for now, imagine you are in a boat floating downstream through magnificent scenery, ultimate destination unknown.

You think you are going to the ocean, but you are not quite sure. You have lost your paddle, so all you can do is hold onto the boat and trust it is going to take you where you are supposed to go.

I know. It sounds like I'm asking you to give up control of your destination. I am.

The only way you can learn to FLOW is by trusting there is something that is guiding your tiny little boat, or that the river knows where it is going.

I can feel some of you rolling your eyes, so let's look at the concept of flow with a little less metaphor.

Our minds are constantly pushing for us to BE more, DO more, HAVE more, and WANT something different. This is how the mind is wired: to keep seeking, learning, changing, and growing.

But most of those mind dictates are actually causing us to live more in an adrenalin state, where the energy is force/push/achieve, instead of in an oxytocin state of flow/allow/receive.

Oxytocin, the hormone of ease and happiness, is an essential element of learning to flow around life's challenges.

Much of life triggers an adrenalin response in our brains. When there is too much adrenalin, our adrenal system gets overly stimulated, which is why so many of us go into burnout when we are moving at the pace of overload.

Piles of clutter can certainly cause this adrenalin response, especially if you trip over those piles or cringe whenever you look their way. *So simplifying your life can actually be a very positive step toward keeping your body healthy!*

You can learn to consciously bring more oxytocin into your life. It can be as simple as deep breathing, laughing, giving hugs, and practicing being in flow.

We live more consistently in a state of flow by slowing down, listening to the whispers, opening space in our schedules to be more spontaneous, and being willing to answer those gentle nudges from our soul that say, *here is where you need to go.*

If you are still working for someone else, this may be more difficult, but there are still ways you can use the concept of flow to work smarter, not harder.

If you are a parent with multiple child-related activities and responsibilities that do not seem to end, teach your children about flow by giving them free play time while you give yourself a bit of essential self-nourishment.

If you are a driven entrepreneur who is either running an empire or still building one, you need to pay attention to flow more than ever. Living in FLOW will keep you from burning out, and it will also take you wherever you are going with more ease.

Of course, everyone has a different flow-state. I normally have to test the extremes (too busy and not busy enough) before I find mine.

The thing that keeps me in FLOW, when I can manage that, is making enough time to pause before every single choice I make, and even in the middle of those choices. It is making sure I am not rushing through my tasks and conversations, but savoring them and infusing them with spaciousness.

I call this The Great Pause because it is one of the absolute essential steps in learning how to move, as my vision-partner Vasi Huntalas says, from Force to Flow.

And it begins with being willing to stand still.

simply enough

Stand Still

Most of my life I have been driven, motivated by a vision to contribute to a world that I felt was missing something important that I was intended to give.

All those years, I believed I was not reaching my full potential if I was not setting stretch goals, testing my limits, filling my days with constant motion and movement toward some future person I was becoming.

It took a lot of standing still to find what I was missing.

I still move. I am still moved to create and to give where I can with what I have. Yet I am mostly motivated by a different force, an inner quiet, that moves me in a different way than it sometimes appears others are being moved.

To be honest, I don't have that many external goals and desires any more. I am simply beholding the wonder of the world as it moves me into the next beautiful moment.

Sometimes I judge myself for this. *Am I doing enough? Shouldn't I have more passion and enthusiasm? Have I given up on humanity, or myself? Is my thyroid out of balance again?* <grin>

Sometimes I buy back into thinking I need something I do not already have. But, rather than give in to the voices, my commitment to stillness and spaciousness has grown.

I am not afraid of standing still.

With all the turmoil in the outside world, we need stillness more than ever.

If you are moving into a simpler life, searching for more meaning as you follow the less-is-more approach to living, stillness is essential. If you are driven by goals and trying to catch the next wave of accomplishment, stillness is even more essential.

Do not be afraid to stand still.

Be afraid of moving so fast that you miss your life. Be afraid of getting lost in the currents of somebody else's life. Be afraid of moving past the golden moments where your Real Life is happening.

As David Whyte says in his poem, Lost: *"Stand still. The forest knows where you are. You must let it find you."*

Be afraid of missing the deeper connections that will happen when you stop long enough to let them find you.

Stop being afraid to stand still.

And when you stop being afraid, when you begin finding joy in the stillness, you may discover that everything is more simple and clear than before.

When you bring adequate stillness into your life, your actions will spring from a consciousness that could not find you when you were rushing around in fear of missing some diamond hidden in the forest of your life.

The diamond is right here, in the Center of YOU.

Be Still. Let life find you.

The simple life
comes from great inner peace.

Inner peace comes through ongoing choice:
Dwell in Presence
or be carried away by every outer storm.

A deep letting go into inner stillness,
equally symphonic and utterly quiet,
a frequency beyond sound.

This is the simplicity that will carry you
into the wide-awake ocean
of your radiant becoming.

Choose to empty.
Be peace full.

Choose to Be Free

"It takes a lot of courage to release the familiar and seemingly secure, to embrace the new. But there is no real security in what is no longer meaningful. There is more security in the adventurous and exciting, for in movement there is life, and in change there is power."
–Alan Cohen

When I started my simplification journey, I wasn't thinking of myself as courageous, but it does take courage to follow the heart into a simpler life, especially when we are on a different track than our friends and family. It takes both courage and ongoing choice to stay on the simplicity track.

What I did not expect was how freeing it would be to even make the choice to have less, and how my spirit would begin to soar just taking that first step on this new life adventure.

As I continue to choose less-is-more, especially after I slip up and buy back into the more-is-more mindset for a short while, I always-always-always feel so unencumbered and free.

The Cohen quote says security is in the adventure and that there is power in change, but I believe security comes from within and that we build resilience by *embracing* change, which leads to our inner power (i.e. empowerment).

To me, this is what freedom is about: being empowered to choose, then knowing I have the capacity to follow that choice.

Most of us in the modern world have the freedom to choose, even if we don't exercise it. *How many people do you know who have lost their inner glow while hanging on to the perceived security of a job or life situation they have simply outgrown?*

simply enough

It doesn't serve anyone to hold on when it is time to let go.

Perhaps the most compelling reason to let go of excess is that it requires us to keep choosing what we truly need to be even more free.

So if you think freedom is something you will have after you pay off your mortgage, have more money in the bank, are finally able to leave your soul-sucking job, start by simply choosing to be free of some of your stuff.

You never know where that simple choice will take you.

Freedom is a persistent opening,
embracing life as it moves you
exactly where you are meant to be.

Unattached to outcome.

Open to possibility.

Reflect: Where does my life feel spacious?

You have made it to the destination point in this book, but you are alive, so your life is still your journey.

There will be times that flow with ease and grace, and times that will not. The more you connect with the flowing times, the easier it will be to repeat them.

If you are someone who is always busy and is uncomfortable with stillness, it might be extra important for you to sit with these questions to see what you find.

Consider where your life feels simple, spacious, and free...and where it could use a little (or a lot) more flow.

What does freedom look like to me...and where do I still feel attached or not free?

When have I experienced being in a state of flow and where is this most present in my life now?

What keeps me in this flow state?

What interrupts my flow?

Death and the Ultimate Letting Go

"For a star to be born, there is one thing that must happen: a gaseous nebula must collapse. So collapse. Crumble. This is not your destruction. This is your birth." -Enjolas

The topic of death might not seem like a good way to end this book, but it IS an essential part of finding your way to staying more free of attachments. Because, when you think about your imminent passing from this world, you are unlikely to consider all the stuff you want to take with you.

So thinking about death is actually one of the best ways to get totally honest with what you truly want to keep. If you were to die today, what would you take with you? What would you most like to leave behind?

If you have lost someone close to you, you will know there is a complex mixture of emotions around this topic of ultimate letting go. On one side, we want to keep physical mementos of our loved ones, a way to save the heart of what we remember about them. On the other side, there is often a whole lot of clutter to clear before we can even get close to that heart.

When my in-laws moved into assisted living, I had first-hand experience of what it is like to deal with those layers. It took months of clearing, and there are still a couple of boxes of old photos tucked in my husband's side of the garage.

Then I had a few friends die suddenly, and all those layers of collecting and saving seemed to collide in a firm commitment to further simplify. When we are in touch with the essence of our own life and choose to keep only what nourishes that, it will be much simpler for our loved ones to deal with those layers of

simply enough

letting go (and, trust me, this can be a greater act of love than leaving a large inheritance).

But there is another side to the death conversation: as you let go of layers of old belongings and beliefs, it may actually feel like a part of you is dying. When you begin to release layers of excess to get to the essence of your life, parts of you will absolutely need to die before you can completely let go.

Like a star, this is an important part of the birth of your new radiance.

This dimension of dying is about allowing the natural cycles of life to collapse the old so the new can shine through.

It isn't always comfortable being a star, but we are a necessary part of life's constantly re-birthing constellation, and we are being called to live more boldly and expansively than ever before.

The world is waking up and it is time for us to plant ourselves even more firmly in who we are, as individuals and as significant parts of the communities in which we live; time to remove all the cloudy layers that are hiding that core brilliance.

When layers of excess cover our inner brilliance, we don't shine.

The star knows this. So does a caterpillar. It must die to the old before it can ever become a butterfly.

To live is to be slowly born.

-Antoine de Sait-Exupery

Emergence

What would it be like to be a caterpillar, to actually spin yourself into a cocoon in preparation for the next transformation? Is the caterpillar aware of her next emergence as a beautiful butterfly, or does she simply do what she knows she must do?

Perhaps the caterpillar knows in her cells that the next step in her transformation is to simply let go. So she stops eating, starts spinning, and pretty soon is enclosed in darkness.

Can you imagine consciously choosing to go there? Me neither. But, for the caterpillar, the dark place is where the true transformation happens.

At first, the old caterpillar cells try to hang on. The caterpillar's immune system actually devours the new butterfly cells (called imaginal cells) in a valiant attempt to stay the same. But the imaginal cells begin to cluster, becoming stronger together than any of the individual cells, old or new.

Fortunately for the butterfly, these imaginal cells figure out that by being a community, a tribe of courageous new explorers, they are able to birth a totally new reality.

Did the caterpillar envision itself as this glorious creature with wings? Probably not, but this is what her Design is meant to be.

Imagine that within each human there lives both a caterpillar and a butterfly. Our first task would be to simply emerge through the various stages of metamorphosis to find, and spread, our wings. Our choice, as we grow, is whether to feed the lowly bug habits or to rise into the magnificence of our becoming.

Being awake is allowing the emergence to keep happening,

even when we feel like diving back into the cocoon.

What is next, after we begin to awaken to the possibility that we are something more than this shell we call a body? Are we, in fact, the imaginal cells of God here to awaken a whole new earth?

Perhaps it is time to gather in another way, as Nori Huddle shares in her beautiful poem, The Imaginal Cell Story:

> *Since the butterfly now "knows" that it is a butterfly,*
> *the little tiny imaginal cells no longer have to do all*
> *those things individual cells must do.*
>
> *Now they are part of a multi-celled organism—a*
> *FAMILY who can share the work.*
>
> *Each new butterfly cell can take on a different job.*
> *There is something for everyone to do.*
>
> *And everyone is important. And each cell begins to do*
> *just that very thing it is most drawn to do. And every*
> *other cell encourages it to do just that.*

If you knew you were one of the imaginal cells creating a whole new entity more beautiful than you could possibly imagine, what would you claim as your part in the great emergence?

Would it start with letting go of some of the excess in your life?

Want simple change?
Create a simplicity habit.

Practice: Choose Simplicity Habits

Now that you have more awareness and a deeper connection to what is most essential in your life, it will take commitment to do the heavy lifting and keep clearing the non-essential that will create lasting change. It will take practice, a bit of discipline, and ongoing choice to be free.

You may not love organizing like I do, but making time to create a spacious life can be both joyful and simple if you decide to like it. Once you feel the benefits of having more space and freedom, you may even start loving the process.

Here are a few simple things you can do to begin cultivating simplicity habits. I have more comprehensive checklists on my website, as well as group mentoring support if you need it.

Create a Daily Surface Clearing Practice.

These daily habits will help keep your ongoing clutter from getting out of control. Do them morning or evening, whatever works best for your rhythm.

Home/Office: pick up your clothes, make your bed, clear the counters and sink, wash the dishes, organize incoming mail (recycle or put into an action basket), read and answer important messages by email, text, phone.

Mind/Body/Spirit: choose a "meditate-motivate-move" routine, and do it often enough to make it a habit. End every day counting your blessings and giving thanks.

simply enough

Schedule a Weekly Clutter-Clearing session

Home: do the laundry, home care essentials, and clear clutter, one box at a time.

Mind-Body: release, relax, renew...take one tech-free day every weekend.

Office/Computer: clear incoming email and messages, moving your inbox to save/follow-up folders (if you can't manage this every week, then get off some of your lists); clear your paper by sorting into recycle/act/save baskets.

Take Simplicity Breaks

Set your timer...at least 3 times every day. When it goes off, take 3 deep breaths, stretch your body, drink a glass of water.

Take a Simplification Sabbatical...at least once every year. Go somewhere simple and sacred, or stay home with an empty calendar. Create space to really go through physical, technology, photos, books, jewelry, etc. Breathe new life into your life.

The Deeper Questions

How can I cultivate a more flowing, meaning full life?

Where can I use more stillness in my life?

What am I afraid might happen if I stay TOO still?

Endings

& New Beginnings

Are we there yet? Remember...

the joy is in the journey.

You have a voice inside
that speaks louder
than the noise in the outer world.
To hear its simple wisdom,
you must be still.

Quiet your thoughts
for one round moment of time.
Then go back, as the center still point
to the middle of your life's endless whirl.

But for now, just sit.

Your heart beating is real. Listen.
The wind on your skin is real. Feel.
Your eyes are awake. See.

Your hands are capable and strong. Use them.

Your mind is creative. Open it.

Your heart is compassionate. Fill it.

You have everything you need
to give what this world needs from you.

What you have is inside,
waiting for permission to shine.

So go out into the world and be the sanity,
be the love, be as real as you dare to be.

This is how we change the world,
one person at a time.

Begin Now.

The Questions (A Summary)

Gathering

This is where we begin to uncover some of the layers by looking at where they came from. Consider the treasures you found as you reflected upon what you have already gathered. Whatever you found, celebrate all of it! This is what has made you who you are today. Continue reflecting...

Which of my belongings make me most happy?

What do my physical possessions say about me?

Are any no longer aligned with who I am becoming?

Sorting

This is the essence of what you will keep and what matters most where you are in your life right now. It will keep changing, so keep sorting. Free some of those limiting beliefs...

Where in my life was there enough...and where was there lack?

When did I feel most free and happy...and how did those parts of my life impact my beliefs about having or being enough?

Are any of those stories/beliefs causing me to hang onto more than I need? What do I really need?

simply enough

Holding On

Where we explore the energy of contraction, holding too tightly, and what can happen when we open our giving flow. Did you find any places you were holding too tightly? Keep opening!

Which areas feel cluttered and messy, and which feel most light and spacious?

Where am I holding on most tightly, and where might it help to loosen my grip?

How is it serving me to keep holding on?

Letting Go

Where we look at when enough is 'too much' and what we are ready to release to create a more spacious life. Whatever you have let go of is *enough* (for now)! Continue...

Where is my stuff getting in the way of my efficiency and productivity?

What am I holding onto that might be of use to someone else?

How might more spaciousness in (name an area) create more freedom?

Abundance

This is the phase we connect with the energy of 'more than enough' and begin to celebrate life's simple abundance. Keep practicing your gratitude and generosity as you notice...

What does abundance look and feel like to me?

Where do I already have enough, and more than enough, in my life?

Do I have any areas of over-gathering (or giving) that are breaking my natural flow?

Flow

The final phase is the place of 'simply enough' where life feels spacious and free, and we have everything we need...at least in THIS moment. It will keep changing, so keep considering...

What does freedom look like to me? Where do I still feel attached or not free?

When have I experienced being in a state of flow and where is this most present in my life now?

What keeps me in this flow state? What interrupts my flow?

Which Simplicity Habits
will you keep?

Gratitude

My first appreciation goes to you, for joining me on your journey to a more simple, meaningful life by reading this book. I hope you were able to gain some insight, and that you will continue to integrate some of these practices into your life.

I am always grateful for my vision-partner, Vasi, who listens with unending patience and laser-like focus to guide me deeper and celebrate my successes. Thank you, my forever friend.

I have a badass writing mentor who helped merge two books into one and get to the heart of what wanted to be written. Stacy, I appreciate you being there for the beginning.

Jennifer, your ability to capture my vision with a design continues to astonish me. Thank you for playing, again, my friend.

My marketing partner at Sacred Stories Publishing helped me get clear on publishing choices, even though I chose to self-publish this book. Patricia, I so appreciate your belief in me, this book, and my other writing, and I am so grateful for all of the connections you are already making on my behalf!

I had a small group of book angels who not only helped me fine-tune and simplify this book, but also believed in me and this project when I was ready to let go of needing to see it published. Beth, Lora, Cathy, Gail, Elizabeth, Petalyn, Nancy, David, Max, Eden...you are the wind beneath the wings of this book, and I am grateful to each of you. Thank you for your input, and for your faith in me.

Garet, you are also the wind beneath my wings, in life and in love. Thank you for always being ready to cheer me on and wait patiently while I am in my focusing & finishing mode.

simply enough

Although he doesn't know it, my grandson also helped inform this book and inspire my commitment to a more simple, flowing life. When I first met him, my heart filled with awe and I knew it would never be the same. Kashus, you are my more-than-enough.

Even though they are not on the same simplicty path as their mama, my grown children constantly teach me about letting go of what is no longer important, as they remind me to focus on what is. Katie and Austin, you inspire me more than you know.

Finally, though there is really no end to gratitude, is there? I am eternally grateful to my spiritual mentor, Annam, for showing me the place of *more-than-enough* as she guides me through so many layers of egoic letting go.

Here I am, again, full of Love.

Sora Garrett is a highly-creative humanitarian who spent years resisting her identity as an organizational genie. After becoming burnt out trying to change the world, she decided to focus on shining light on what is good in her world while helping you create joy and meaning in yours.

Still passionate about creating a better world, her business is a philanthropy playground where she gives a portion of every product or program to support collaborative giving programs that are creating grassroots change.

With over 30 years of business experience, from corporate to non-profit to self-employed, Sora brings a broad systems perspective to her work as a creative organizer. She is both a spiritual seeker and humanitarian activist, inviting her readers to open to the bigger reasons we are here as we join together for real-world change.

Sora lives in Star, Idaho. When she is not writing or creating, she enjoys traveling, gardening, walking, skiing, and sharing time with her husband of 40+ years, their two grown children, one amazing grandson, and a mini-schnauzer named Emma-Joy.

simply enough

Dear Readers,

I have so many favorite resources, and they are always changing, so instead of listing them here, I invite you to check out the resources page on my website, soragarrett.com.

You will also find a Joyful Simplicity focusing system that will help you create good simplicity habits, as well as simplicity support groups for gentle guidance, accountability, and friendship!

While you are at my website, please sign up for the Simply Shine e-letter, and check out my other books and free e-books.

I love inspiring you on your journey to a more spacious, joyful, meaningful life!

Other books by Sora

The Miracle Keys

Ignite Your Inner Star

Silent Grace

Join the Joyful Simplicity Club on Facebook,
where you will find joymates &
group experiences for your journey
to a life of Simply Enough.

Find other resources and support at:
soragarrett.com

This book is available in special quantity discount
for simplicity groups and book clubs.

Please contact the author at:
shine@soragarrett.com

Made in the USA
Columbia, SC
13 November 2021

48856346R00096